CATULLUS:
LOVE AND HATE

CATULLUS: LOVE AND HATE

SELECTED SHORT POEMS

EDITED WITH NOTES
AND RUNNING VOCABULARIES

BY

LEO M. KAISER

BOLCHAZY-CARDUCCI PUBLISHERS

COVER BY LEON DANILOVICS

This book was digitized via the Kurzweil scanner and typeset on Quadex 5000 and Compugraphic 8600 at Chicago Scan Typographers, Inc. a division of Bolchazy-Carducci Publishers, Inc.

© Copyright 1986
Reprint 1993
Bolchazy-Carducci Publishers
1000 Brown Street
Wauconda, IL 60084 U.S.A.

Printed in the United States of America

International Standard Book Number
0-86516-180-1

Parentibus meis

CONTENTS

Preface

One of the most charming of ancient Roman poets is C. Valerius Catullus. Among the numerous modern accolades of scholars are characterizations of him as "the greatest lyrical poet of Rome" (Eric Arthur Barber); "a poet of exquisite pathos and tenderness" (Thomas William Melluish); "the most passionate and brilliant, if not the greatest, of Roman poets" (Arthur Palmer); "patron saint of poets of love, unsurpassed in sheer beauty of description of the lovely and the tender" (Karl Pomeroy Harrington); "the clearest, if not the richest, poet-voice ever lifted in Rome" (Elmer Truesdell Merrill).

To introduce such a poet to Latin students at the earliest feasible stage is the aim of this simple libellus with its notes, visible vocabularies, and various poetic materials. The editor trusts the encounter may be one often repeated.

A recent bilingual edition of all the poems of Catullus is G. P. Goold, *Catullus* (London: Duckworth, 1983). For several phrasings I am indebted to the editions of F. W. Cornish, Robinson Ellis, and E. T. Merrill, the last a model of annotation.

L.M.K.

Introduction

Catullus (84-54 B.C.) was born in northern
Italy at Verona, roughly midway between Milan
and Venice, to a wealthy and distinguished
father who was a friend of Julius Caesar. Like
many promising youths from outlying regions,
he was attracted by the feverish glitter of the
capital, and in his early twenties removed to
Rome to complete his education and to
become part of fashionable society. He made
numerous friends and some enemies by his
personal charm and by his frankness.

Almost immediately he fell under the spell
of the beautiful but unprincipled Clodia, the
Lesbia of his poems, wife of the consul Q.
Metellus Celer—later poisoned, some whis-
pered, by her—and perhaps sister of Cicero's
bitter enemy, the tribune P. Clodius Pulcher.
Clodia proved as fickle to Catullus as to her
other lovers. Knowing her unfaithful, he vacil-
lated still between love and hate, his unhappi-
ness compounded by news of his brother's
death in the Troad. Eventually he achieved a
renunciation.

One year of his life he spent in Asia Minor
on the staff of the governor of Bithynia; on the
way back to Rome he visited his brother's

grave in the Troad. The last years of his life he seems to have passed in Rome except for visits to Verona, and to Tibur and Sirmio where he had villas.

While the poems that describe his love affair with Clodia represent some of his best known and finest pieces, placing him along with Sappho and Shelley among the greatest lyric poets of the world, Catullus produced much else of the highest order—elegy, epigram, wedding songs, and long scholarly poems in imitation of Hellenistic poetry—differing widely in language, tone and style. Some of his poems are lost, but those that survive amount to over two thousand lines, an impressive output for one who died so young.

On Catullus

Tell me not what too well I know
About the bard of Sirmio...
   Yes, in Thalia's son
Such stains there are...as when a Grace
Sprinkles another's laughing face
   With nectar, and runs on.

Walter Savage Landor

2. Pretty Poll

Passer, deliciae meae puellae,
quicum ludere, quem in sinu tenere
cui primum digitum dare appetenti
et acres solet incitare morsus
5 cum desiderio meo nitenti
carum nescio quid libet iocari,
(credo) ut, cum gravis acquiescet ardor,
sit solaciolum sui doloris—
tecum ludere sicut ipsa possem
10 et tristes animi levare curas!

METER: hendecasyllabic (- -/-xx/-x/-x/-x).

INFLUENCE: Skelton, "Boke of Phyllyp Sparowe";
Cranstoun, "Sparrow! My Darling's Joy";
Gascoigne, "The Praise of Philip Sparrow";
Cartright, "Lesbia on Her Sparrow."

NOTES: 1 passer: vocative. puellae: Lesbia.
2 quicum: quocum (cum quo). ludere: this and
the other infinitives in lines 2-4 are dependent
upon solet, the verb for the three relative
clauses. 3 primum digitum: "finger-tip". appetenti: "as it pecks". 4 (Lesbia) solet. 5
cum: "when". desiderio meo nitenti: Lesbia;
dat. after libet. 6 nescio quid carum: "some
game or other"; object of iocari. 7 ardor
(amoris). 9 possem: "would I were able".

passer, eris, m. sparrow
deliciae, arum delight
ludo, 3, lusi, lusum play
sinus, us, m. lap
primus, a, um first
digitus, i finger
appeto, 3, appetii, appetitum
   grasp at
acer, acris, acre sharp
soleo, 2, solitus be accustomed
incito, 1 provoke
morsus, us, m. bite
5 desiderium, ii desire
nitens, entis shining, beautiful
carus, a, um dear
nescio quis, nescio quid some
   one or other, something
   or other

libet, 2, libuit it pleases
iocor, 1 play
credo, 3, credidi, creditum
   believe
gravis, e grievous
acquiesco, 3, acquievi,
   acquietum abate
ardor, oris, m. ardor
solaciolum, i consolation
dolor, oris, m. grief
sicut just as
10 tristis, e gloomy
levo, 1 lighten
cura, ae care

HARTLEY COLERIDGE

Little Sparrow, Pretty Sparrow

Little sparrow, pretty sparrow,
Darling of my 'winsome marrow,'
Plaything, playmate, what you will,
Tiny love, or naughty Phil,
Tempted, teased, to peck and hop
On her slender finger top,
Free to nuzzle and to rest
In the sweet valley of her breast;
Her wee, wee comfort in her sorrow's wane,
When sinks to sleep the fever of her pain...

3. Poor Poll

Lugete, o Veneres Cupidinesque,
et quantum est hominum venustiorum.
Passer mortuus est meae puellae,
passer, deliciae meae puellae,
5 quem plus illa oculis suis amabat:
nam mellitus erat suamque norat
ipsam tam bene quam puella matrem;
nec sese a gremio illius movebat,
sed, circumsiliens modo huc modo illuc,
10 ad solam dominam usque pipiabat.
Qui nunc it per iter tenebricosum
illuc, unde negant redire quemquam.
At vobis male sit, malae tenebrae
Orci, quae omnia bella devoratis:
15 tam bellum mihi passerem abstulistis.
Vae factum male! vae miselle passer!
Tua nunc opera meae puellae
flendo turgiduli rubent ocelli.

METER: hendecasyllabic (- -/-xx/-x/-x/-x).

INFLUENCE: Skelton, "Book of Phyllyp Sparowe";
Drummond, "On the Death of a Linnet."

NOTES: 2 quantum est: "as many as there are".
6 suamque: with ipsam: "his own mistress". norat:
noverat. 11 Qui: Hic. 12 negant quemquam: "they
say that no one". 13 vobis male sit: "a curse on you".

lugeo, 2, luxi, luctum mourn
Venus, neris, f. Grace, Charm
Cupido, dinis, f. Love
quantus, a, um as many as
venustus, a, um graceful,
 charming
passer, eris, m. sparrow
morior, 3, mortuus die
deliciae, arum delight
6 mellitus, a, um honey-sweet
novi, novisse know
tam bene quam as well as
gremium, ii lap
circumsilio, 4 hop about
modo now
huc hither
illuc thither
10 solus, a, um alone
domina, ae mistress
usque ever
pipio, 1 chirp
eo, ire, ii, itum go

tenebricosus, a, um
 dark, gloomy
unde from which
redeo, redire, redii, reditum
 return
quisquam, quidquam
 anyone, anything
malus, a, um evil, cruel
tenebrae, arum darkness
Orcus, i Orcus, Hades
bellus, a, um pretty
devoro, 1 devour
15 aufero, auferre, abstuli,
 ablatum carry off
vae ah!
misellus, a, um wretched little
opera, ae doing
fleo, 2, flevi, fletum weep
turgidulus, a, um swollen little
rubeo, 2 be red
ocellus, i little eye, dear eye

ROBERT HERRICK

from Upon the Death of His Sparrow

Phil, the late dead, the late dead dear,
O! may no eye distil a tear
For you once lost, who weep not here!
Had Lesbia, too-too kind, but known
This sparrow, she had scorned her own,
And for this dead which under lies
Wept out her heart, as well as eyes.

6

5. Kiss and Don't Tell

Vivamus, mea Lesbia, atque amemus,
rumoresque senum severiorum
omnes unius aestimemus assis.
Soles occidere et redire possunt:
5 nobis cum semel occidit brevis lux,
nox est perpetua una dormienda.
Da mi basia mille, deinde centum,
dein mille altera, dein secunda centum,
deinde usque altera mille, deinde centum.
10 Dein, cum milia multa fecerimus,
conturbabimus illa, ne sciamus,
aut ne quis malus invidere possit,
cum tantum sciat esse basiorum.

METER: hendecasyllabic (- -/-xx/-x/-x/-x).

INFLUENCE: Marlowe, "The Passionate Shepherd
to His Love"; Campion, Song, in "Book of Airs";
Jonson, "The Forest"; Prior, "Ode to Celia".

NOTES: 3 unius assis: "at a single farthing".
4-6 Some of the most poignant lines in Latin
poetry. 5 occidit: pres. perf. lux: the
monosyllable at the end of the lines intensifies
the idea of finality. 7 deinde: pronounce through-
out as two syllables, dein as a monosyllable. 10
fecerimus: fut. perf. 13 According to Roman super-
stition, detailed knowledge about another person
enabled one to exert the evil eye upon him.

vivo, 3, vixi, victum live
Lesbia, ae Lesbia (Clodia),
   C.'s lover
rumor, oris, m. talk
senex, senis, m. old man
severus, a, um strict
aestimo, 1 value
as,assis, m. farthing
sol,solis, m. sun
occido, 3, occidi, occasum
   set, perish
redeo, redire, redii,
   reditum return
5 semel once
brevis, e brief
lux, lucis, f. light, day
perpetuus, a, um uninterrupted

dormio, 4, dormii, dormitum
   sleep
mi = mihi
basium, ii kiss
mille thousand; milia thousands
deinde then
centum a hundred
dein = deinde
secundus, a, um following
usque without pause
11 conturbo, 1 mix up the
   number of
scio, 4, scii, scitum know
quis, quid anyone, anything
invideo, 2, invidi, invisum look
   on with evil eye

BEN JONSON

To Celia

Come, my Celia, let us prove,
While wee can, the sports of love;
Time will not be ours for ever:
He, at length, our goods will sever.
Spend not then his gifts in vaine.
Sunnes that set may rise againe;
But, if once wee lose this light,
'Tis, with us, perpetuall night.
Why should wee deferre our joyes?
Fame and rumor are but toies.
Cannot wee delude the eyes
Of a few poore houshold spyes?
Or his easier eares beguile,
So removed by our wile?
'Tis no sinne love's fruit to steale;
But the sweet thefts to reveale:
To bee taken, to be seene,
These have crimes accounted beene.

8. She Loves Me Not

Miser Catulle, desinas ineptire,
et quod vides perisse perditum ducas.
Fulsere quondam candidi tibi soles,
cum ventitabas quo puella ducebat
5 amata nobis quantum amabitur nulla.
Ibi illa multa tum iocosa fiebant,
quae tu volebas nec puella nolebat.
Fulsere vere candidi tibi soles.
Nunc iam illa non vult: tu quoque, impotens, noli,
10 nec quae fugit sectare, nec miser vive,

METER: choliambic (x-/x-/x-/x-/x-/-x)

INFLUENCE: Thomas Campion, Imitation; Cowley,
"Love Given Over"; Jonson, "Love Freed from
Folly"; Thomas Carew, "The Mournfull Partyng
of Two Lovers, Caused by the Disproportion
of Estates."

NOTES: 1 desinas: like ducas in line 2, jussive
subjunctive. In this poem Catullus refers to
himself in the first, second, and third persons.
2 perditum ducas: "account as lost". 3 Fulsere: Fulserunt. 4 puella: Lesbia. 5 nobis: mihi (dat. of agency). nulla (puella).
6 Ibi tum: "there and then" (Cornish). 9
illa: Lesbia. Nunc iam: "Now at last" (Ellis). 10 (eam) quae. miser: "in misery".

miser, a, um wretched
Catullus, i Catullus
desino, 3, desii, desitum cease
ineptio, 4 play the fool
pereo, perire, perii, peritum
  perish
perdo, 3, perdidi, perditum lose
duco, 3, duxi, ductum account,
  consider
fulgeo 2, fulsi shine
quondam once
candidus, a, um bright
sol, solis, m. sun
ventito, 1 be wont to come

quo whither
5 quantum as much as
ibi there
tum then
iocosus, a, um merry
fio, fieri, factus happen
volo, velle, volui wish
nolo, nolle, nolui not to wish
vere truly
impotens, entis, m. weakling
10 fugio, 3, fugi, fugitum flee
sector, 1 pursue
vivo, 3, vixi, victum live

SIR THOMAS WYATT

My Lute Awake

Perchaunce the lye wethered and old
The wynter nyghtes that are so cold,
Playnyng in vain unto the mone;
Thy wisshes then dare not be told;
Care then who lyst, for I have done.

And then may chaunce the to repent
The tyme that thou hast lost and spent
To cause thy lovers sigh and swoune;
Then shalt thou knowe beaultie but lent,
And wisshe and want as I have done....

sed obstinata mente perfer, obdura.
Vale, puella! Iam Catullus obdurat,
nec te requiret nec rogabit invitam:
at tu dolebis, cum rogaberis nulla,
15 scelesta, nocte. Quae tibi manet vita?
Quis nunc te adibit? Cui videberis bella?
Quem nunc amabis? Cuius esse diceris?
Quem basiabis? Cui labella mordebis?
At tu, Catulle, destinatus obdura.

---

14 nulla nocte: abl. of time. 15 scelesta:
vocative. 17 Cuius esse diceris: "Who will
call you his own?" (Merrill). 18 Cui: dat.
of possession. mordebis: prompted by love.

On Catullus
With him died the clearest, if not the richest,
poet-voice ever lifted in Rome....He delighted
in life with a vigorous animal passion. Not
without charm to him was nature in her sylvan
aspect, yet his highest enjoyment was in the life
of men. And this life he did not study, as did
Horace, from the standpoint of a philosopher.
Indeed, he did not study it at all, but simply
felt it. For he was not outside of it, but a
part of it to the fullest degree, swayed by its
ever-changing emotions.
E. T. Merrill

obstinatus, a, um firmly
    resolved
perfero, perferre, pertuli,
    perlatum endure
obduro, 1 be firm
vale farewell!
requiro, 3, requisivi, requisitum
    seek
invitus, a, um unwilling
doleo, 2, dolui grieve, be sorry
15 scelestus, a, um wretched

qui, quae, quod what
    (interrog. adj.)
quis, quid who, what
    (interrog. pron.)
adeo, adire, adii, aditum visit
bellus, a, um pretty
basio 1 kiss
labellum, i lip
mordeo, 2, momordi,
    morsum bite
destinatus, a, um resolved

THOMAS CAREW

To My Inconstant Mistress

When thou, poor excommunicate
From all the joyes of loves, shall see
The full reward and glorious fate
Which my strong faith shall purchase me,
Then curse thine own inconstancie....

Then shalt thou weepe, entreat, complaine
To Love as I did once to thee;
When all thy teares shall be as vaine
As mine were then; for thou shalt bee
Damn'd for thy false apostasie.

13. Nosegay

Cenabis bene, mi Fabulle, apud me
paucis, si tibi di favent, diebus,
si tecum attuleris bonam atque magnam
cenam, non sine candida puella
5 et vino et sale et omnibus cachinnis.
Haec si, inquam, attuleris, venuste noster,
cenabis bene: nam tui Catulli
plenus sacculus est aranearum.
Sed contra accipies meros amores
10 seu quid suavius elegantiusve est:
nam unguentum dabo, quod meae puellae
donarunt Veneres Cupidinesque;
quod tu cum olfacies, deos rogabis
totum ut te faciant, Fabulle, nasum.

METER: hendecasyllabic (- -/-xx/-x/-x/-x).

INFLUENCE: Martial, 3,12; Jonson, "Cynthia's
Revels", IV,3; John Weever, "Epigrammes in
the Oldest Cut", no. 9.

NOTES: 4 candida puella: a music girl. 9 meros amores: "the essence of delight" (i.e.,
the unguentum). 10 "Or something, if there
be such, still sweeter or choicer". 11 unguentum: employed liberally at feasts. puellae: Lesbia. 12 donarunt: donaverunt.

ceno, 1 dine
bene well
mi voc. masc. sing. of meus
Fabullus, i Fabullus, friend
  of Catullus
apud me at my house
paucus, a, um (pl.) few
deus, i god
faveo, 2, favi, fautum
  be favorable
affero, afferre, attuli, allatum
  bring along
cena, ae dinner
candidus, a, um fair
5 vinum, i wine
sal, salis, m. salt, wit
cachinnus, i laughter
inquam, inquii say
venustus, a, um charming

plenus, a, um full
sacculus, i purse
aranea, ae cobweb
contra in return
accipio, 3, accepi,
  acceptum get
merus, a, um pure, unmixed
seu or if
quis, quid anyone, anything
10 suavis, e sweet
elegans, antis choice
-ve or
unguentum, i perfume
dono, 1 give
Venus, neris, f. Grace, Charm
Cupido, dinis, f. Love
olfacio, 3, olfeci, olfactum smell
totus, a, um all
nasus, i nose

ROBERT HERRICK

The Invitation

...Beere small as comfort, dead as charity.
At which amaz'd, and pondring on the food,
How cold it was, and how it child my blood;
I curst the master; and I damn'd the souce;
And swore I'de got the ague of the house.
Well, when to eat thou dost me next desire,
I'le bring a fever; since thou keep'st no fire.

14

31. O Lovely Sirmio!

Paene insularum, Sirmio, insularumque
ocelle, quascumque in liquentibus stagnis
marique vasto fert uterque Neptunus,
quam te libenter quamque laetus inviso,
5 vix mi ipse credens Thyniam atque Bithynos
liquisse campos et videre te in tuto!
O quid solutis est beatius curis,
cum mens onus reponit, ac peregrino
labore fessi venimus larem ad nostrum
10 desideratoque acquiescimus lecto?
Hoc est, quod unum est pro laboribus tantis.
Salve, o venusta Sirmio, atque ero gaude;
gaudete vosque, o Lydiae lacus undae;
ridete, quidquid est domi cachinnorum.

METER: choliambic (x-/x-/x-/x-/x-/-x).

INFLUENCE: M. A. Flaminio, "To the Muse of Sirmio";
Herrick, "The Plaudite"; Milton, "In Salmasium", 1-7.

NOTES: 2 ocelle: "jewel". 3 uterque Neptunus: god
of both pools and oceans. 6 Supply me as subject
for liquisse and videre. 7 solutis curis: abl. of
comparison. 8 peregrino labore: "the toil of foreign travel". 11 "This alone is reward enough for
such great toil". 12 ero gaude: "make cheer for your
master." 13 Lydiae: the Etruscans, thought to be of
Lydian origin, had early settlements in the region.

paene insula, ae peninsula
Sirmio, onis, f. a promontory
  projecting into the Lake
  of Garda
ocellus, i little eye
quicumque, quaecumque,
  quodcumque whoever,
  whatever
liquens, entis liquid, clear
stagnum, i lake
vastus, a, um vast
uterque, utraque, utrumque
  each
Neptunus, i Neptune, god of
  the sea
quam how
libenter willingly
laetus, a, um joyful
inviso, 3, invisi, invisum see
5 vix scarcely
mi = mihi
credo, 3, credidi, creditum trust
Thynia, ae Thynia, on the
  Black Sea
Bithynius, i Bithynian,
  inhabitant of Thrace
linquo, 3, liqui leave
campus, i plain
tutus, a, um safe; in tuto
  in safety
quis, quid who, what?

solutus, a, um set free
beatus, a, um blessed
cura, ae care
onus, oneris, n. burden
repono, 3, reposui, repositum
  put aside
peregrinus, a, um foreign
labor, oris, m. toil
fessus, a, um wearied
lar, laris, m. guardian deity of
  the household, the home
10 desideratus, a, um longed for
acquiesco, 3, acquievi,
  acquietum repose
lectus, i bed
unus, a, um alone
pro a reward for
tantus, a, um such great
salve hail!
venustus, a, um lovely
erus, i master
gaudeo, 2, gavisus rejoice
Lydius, a, um Lydian, Etruscan
lacus, us, m. lake
unda, ae wave
rideo, 2, risi, risum laugh
quisquis, quidquid whoever,
  whatever
domus, us, f. home; domi
  at home
cachinnus, i laughter

43. None So Fair As She

Salve, nec minimo puella naso
nec bello pede nec nigris ocellis
nec longis digitis nec ore sicco
nec sane nimis elegante lingua,
5 decoctoris amica Formiani.
Ten Provincia narrat esse bellam?
Tecum Lesbia nostra comparatur?
O saeclum insapiens et infacetum!

METER: hendecasyllabic (--/-xx/-x/-x/-x).

INFLUENCE: Herrick: "No Loathsomnesse in
Love"; Buchanan, "Iambon Liber", 4; John
Donne, "Elegie VIII."

NOTES: 1 minimo naso: ablative of quality;
so too the ablatives of lines 2-4. puella: vocative; a certain Ameana, a plain
and avaricious woman. 5 decoctoris
Formiani: the notorious Mamurra of Formiae.
6 Ten: Tene, subject of esse, and referring
to Ameana. Provincia: modern Provence.
8 saeclum: saeculum.

Catulli carmina, quotquot supersint, ex-
eunte demum saeculo post Christum natum
tertio decimo ex oblivione in Italorum
studiosorum notitiam prodiisse iam satis
constat; unicum illud exemplar repperisse
(quo in loco nescimus) notarium quendam
Veronensem testatur epigramma Benevenuti
de Campexanis Vicentini—R. A. B. My-
nors, *Catulli Carmina*, Oxonii, MCMLVIII.

salve hello!
minimus, a, um tiny
nasus, i nose
bellus, a, um pretty
niger, gra, grum black
ocellus, i little eye
longus, a, um long
digitus, i finger
os, oris, n. mouth
siccus, a, um dry
sane indeed, surely
nimis very
elegans, antis refined
lingua, ae tongue
5 decoctor, oris, m. bankrupt,
    spendthrift

amica, ae mistress
Formianus, a, um of Formiae,
    the modern town of Mola
    di Gaeta
-ne enclitic indicating
    a question
Provincia, ae the Province
narro, 1 say
Lesbia, ae Lesbia (Clodia)
comparo, 1 compare
saeculum, i age
insapiens, entis tasteless
infacetus, a, um ill bred

From the Sanskrit of Chauras
Even now
I love long black eyes that caress like silk,
Ever and ever sad and laughing eyes,
Whose lids make such sweet shadow when they close
It seems another beautiful look of hers;
I love a fresh mouth, ah, a scented mouth,
And curving hair, subtle as smoke,
And light fingers, and laughter of green gems.
Tr. by E. Powys Mathers

51. Lovesick

Ille mi par esse deo videtur,
ille, si fas est, superare divos,
qui sedens adversus identidem te
    spectat et audit
5 dulce ridentem, misero quod omnes
eripit sensus mihi; nam simul te,
Lesbia, aspexi, nihil est super mi
    vocis in ore,
lingua sed torpet, tenuis sub artus
10 flamma demanat, sonitu suopte
tintinant aures, gemina teguntur
    lumina nocte.

METER: Sapphic (-x/--/-xx/-x/-x)
              (-xx/-x)

INFLUENCE: Wyatt, "What Menythe Thys"; Spenser,
"Amoretti," 39; George Turberville, "On hir I
gazde a whyle"; Sidney, "My muse, what ails this
ardour?" Campion, "O sweet delight, O more than
human bliss."

NOTES: This poem is a free translation of an ode
of Sappho. 2 si fas est (dicere). superare:
depends upon videtur. 5 quod: the antecedent
is the entire fact described in the preceding
lines. 6 mihi: functions both as dat. of possession and a dat. of separation. 7 est super:
superest (tmesis). 11 gemina: a transferred
epithet; logically it should modify lumina.

mi = mihi
par, paris equal, like
fas est it is lawful
supero, 1 surpass
divus, i god
sedeo, 2, sedi, sessum sit
adversus (adv.) opposite
identidem again and again
specto, 1 see
5 dulce sweetly
rideo, 2, risi, risum laugh
miser, a, um wretched
eripio, 3, eripui, ereptum
   take away
sensus, us, m. senses (pl.)
simul as soon as
Lesbia, ae Lesbia, Catullus'
   mistress

aspicio, 3, aspexi, aspectum
   behold
supersum, superesse, superfui
   remain
os, oris, n. mouth
lingua, ae tongue
torpeo, 2, be numb
tenuis, e subtle
artus, us, m. limb
10 flamma, ae flame
demano, 1 stream down
sonitus, us, m. sound
suopte = suo (emphatic)
tintino, 1 ring
auris, is, f. ear
geminus, a, um twin, both
tego, 3, texi, tectum shroud
lumen, minis, n. eye

SIR PHILIP SIDNEY

From Second Eclogues

My muse, what ail's this ardour?
Mine eys be dym, my lyms shake,
My voice is hoarse, my throte scorchte,
My tong to this my roofe cleaves,
My fancy amazde, my thoughtes dull'd,
My harte doth ake, my life faints,
My sowle beginnes to take leave.

65. In the Midst of My Grief

Etsi me assiduo confectum cura dolore
    sevocat a doctis, Hortale, virginibus,
nec potis est dulces Musarum expromere fetus
    mens animi—tantis fluctuat ipsa malis;
5 namque mei nuper Lethaeo gurgite fratris
    pallidulum manans alluit unda pedem,
Troia Rhoeteo quem subter litore tellus
    ereptum nostris obterit ex oculis....
Alloquar, audiero numquam tua facta loquentem?
10   Numquam ego te, vita frater amabilior,
aspiciam posthac? At certe semper amabo,
    semper maesta tua carmina morte canam,

METER: elegiac couplet (-xx/-xx/-xx/-xx/-xx/--)
                          (-xx/-xx/-/-xx/-xx/-)

INFLUENCE: Herrick, "Farwell Frost."

NOTES: 1 dolore: grief over his brother's death.
2 doctis virginibus: the Muses, i.e., literary ac-
tivity. Hortalus was the friend to whom he sent
this poem with a translation from Callimachus.
3 Musarum expromere fetus: to compose original poems. 4 mens animi: "my soul's imagination". With
tantis begins a digression that ends only at line 14.
ipsa: mens. 7 quem: the antecedent is fratris.
9 Alloquar: supply as object te, Catullus' brother.
numquam: modifies audiero and alloquar.

etsi although
assiduus, a, um constant
confectus, a, um worn out
cura, ae care, sorrow
dolor, oris, m. grief
sevoco, 1 call away
doctus, a, um learned
Hortalus, i Hortalus, friend
    of Catullus
virgo, ginis, f. maid, Muse
potis, e able
dulcis, e sweet
Musa, ae Muse
expromo, 3, exprompsi,
    expromptum utter
fetus, us, m. birth
tantus, a, um so great
fluctuo, 1 be tossed about
malum, i evil, misfortune
5 namque for
nuper lately
Lethaeus, a, um Lethaean;
    relating to the river Lethe
    in the underworld or to
    the underworld in general
gurges, gitis, m. stream

pallidulus, a, um pale
mano, 1 flow, creep
alluo, 3, allui wash, lap
unda, ae wave
Troius, a, um Trojan
Rhoeteum, i Rhoeteum, a
    promontory in the Troad
subter (w. abl.) under
litus, toris, n. shore
tellus, uris, f. earth
eripio, 3, eripui, ereptum
    tear away
obtero, 3, obtrivi, obtritum
    crush
oculus, i eye
alloquor, 3, allocutus speak to
factum, i deed, action
loquor, 3, locutus tell
10 amabilis, e beloved
aspicio, 3, aspexi, aspectum
    see, behold
posthac hereafter
certe surely
maestus, a, um sad
carmen, minis, n. song
cano, 3, cecini, cantum sing

"The 'wave' image of lines 5 and 6, perhaps because
it symbolized the *raison d'etre* of his mourning,
seems to have loomed large in Catullus' mind and
governed to an extent his mode of expression in the
twenty-four line poem"—L. M. Kaiser, *CB* 27. 2.

qualia sub densis ramorum concinit umbris
Daulias absumpti fata gemens Ityli.—
15 Sed tamen in tantis maeroribus, Hortale, mitto
haec expressa tibi carmina Battiadae,
ne tua dicta, vagis nequiquam credita ventis,
effluxisse meo forte putes animo,
ut missum sponsi furtivo munere malum
20 procurrit casto virginis e gremio;
quod, miserae oblitae molli sub veste locatum,
dum adventu matris prosilit, excutitur,
atque illud prono praeceps agitur decursu,
huic manat tristi conscius ore rubor.

---

13 qualia: "such (songs) as". 15 sed tamen: here
Catullus returns to his theme after the long digression. 16 carmina: see note to line 2. 17 tua
dicta: Hortalus' request for the translation. vagis…ventis: "as though committed, vainly, to the
straying winds". 19 ut: the comparison is between
Catullus' "forgetting" Hortalus' request and the girl's
forgetting the apple from her lover. furtivo munere: "in the way of a secret gift"; follows upon missum. malum: proverbial lover's gift. 21 quod:
the apple. miserae…locatum: "placed within the
poor thoughtless girl's soft robe". 23 illud: the
apple. 24 huic: dative of possession after ore:
"over her downcast face".

qualis, e such as
densus, a, um thick
ramus, i branch
concino, 3, concinui,
    concentum sing in chorus
umbra, ae shadow
Daulias, adis, f. bird of Daulis:
    Procne. Procne, wife of
    Tereus of Daulis, slew her
    husband's son, Itylus, and
    was changed into a
    nightingale
absumo, 3, absumpsi,
    absumptum kill
fatum, i fate
gemo, 3, gemui, gemitum
    lament
Itylus, i Itylus, son of Tereus
    of Daulis
15 maeror, oris, m. grief
expressus, a, um translated
Battiades, ae, m. Callimachus,
    poet of Cyrene,
    founded by Battus
dictum, i word
vagus, a, um straying,
    wandering
nequiquam in vain
credo, 3, credidi, creditum
    entrust
ventus, i wind

effluo, 3, effluxi slip away
forte perhaps
ut as
sponsus, i betrothed, lover
furtivus, a, um secret
munus, neris, n. gift
malum, i apple
20 procurro, 3, procurri,
    procursum fall forth
castus, a, um chaste
gremium, ii lap
miser, a, um poor
oblitus, a, um thoughtless
mollis, e soft
vestis, is, f. robe
loco, 1 place
dum while
adventus, us, m. coming
prosilio, 4, prosilui leap up
excutio, 3, excussi, excussum
    shake out
pronus, a, um downward
praeceps, cipitis headlong
ago, 3, egi, actum set in motion
decursus, us, m. fall
mano, 1 creep, flow
tristis, e sad
conscius, a, um guilty
os, oris, n. face
rubor, oris, m. blush

72. Love without Liking

Dicebas quondam solum te nosse Catullum,
  Lesbia, nec prae me velle tenere Iovem.
Dilexi tum te non tantum ut vulgus amicam,
  sed pater ut natos diligit et generos.
5 Nunc te cognovi: quare etsi impensius uror,
  multo mi tamen es vilior et levior.
Qui potis est? inquis. Quod amantem iniuria talis
  cogit amare magis, sed bene velle minus.

METER: elegiac couplet (-xx/-xx/-xx/-xx/-xx/--)
                              (-xx/-xx/-/-xx/-xx/-)

INFLUENCE: Herrick, "To His Booke."

NOTES: 1 Dicebas: "You used to say". nosse:
novisse. 2 prae me: "in preference to me".
(te) velle. tenere: "clasp as a husband" (Ellis).
3 non tantum ut: "not so much as", "not merely as".
vulgus (diligit). 4 ut: "as." 5 nunc te cognovi:
Catullus has found out about Lesbia's other loves.
6 multo: abl. degree of difference: "far". 7 Qui =
Quo: "How". potis: in Catullus sometimes the
equivalent of the neuter, pote.

TIBULLUS I,9,31-34
Tunc mihi iurabas nullo te divitis auri
  pondere, non gemmis vendere velle fidem,
non tibi si pretium Campania terra daretur,
  non tibi si Bacchi cura Falernus ager.

quondam in former days
solus, a, um alone
novi, novisse know
Lesbia, ae Lesbia (Clodia)
prae (w. acc.) before
volo, velle, volui wish
teneo, 2, tenui, tentum hold
Iuppiter, Iovis, m. Jupiter
diligo, 3, dilexi, dilectum love
tum then
tantum…quantum so
    much…as
vulgus, i, n. the common sort
amica, ae mistress
natus, i son
gener, i son-in-law
5 cognovi, cognovisse know
quare wherefore
etsi although

impensus, a, um strong,
    vehement
uro, 3, ussi, ustum burn
mi = mihi
tamen nevertheless
vilis, e cheap
levis, e trifling
potis, e possible
inquam (inquis, inquit),
    inquii say
quod because
amans, antis, m. lover
iniuria, ae injury
talis, e such
cogo, 3, coegi, coactum compel
magis more
bene volo, velle, volui wish
    well, like
minus less

WILLIAM WALSH

Translation of Catullus 72

Thou saidst that I alone thy heart cou'd move
And that for me thou wou'dst abandon Jove.
I lov'd thee then, not with a love defil'd,
But as a father loves his only child.
I know thee now, and tho' I fiercelier burn,
Thou art become the object of my scorn.
See what thy falshood gets; I must confess
I love thee more, but I esteem thee less.

76. Cure Me of Love

Si qua recordanti benefacta priora voluptas
  est homini, cum se cogitat esse pium,
nec sanctam violasse fidem, nec foedere in ullo
  divum ad fallendos numine abusum homines,
5 multa parata manent in longa aetate, Catulle,
  ex hoc ingrato gaudia amore tibi.
Nam quaecumque homines bene cuiquam aut
    dicere possunt
  aut facere, haec a te dictaque factaque sunt;
omnia quae ingratae perierunt credita menti.
10   Quare cur tu te iam amplius excrucies?
Quin tu animum offirmas atque istinc teque reducis
  et dis invitis desinis esse miser?

METER: elegiac couplet (-xx/-xx/-xx/-xx/-xx/--)
                            (-xx/-xx/-/-xx/-xx/-)

INFLUENCE: Campion, "Third Book of Airs," 29.

NOTES: 1 qua: modifies voluptas. benefacta priora: object of recordanti. 4 divum: gen. plur.
abusum (esse). 6 ex hoc ingrato amore: follows
upon parata. The love is for Lesbia. 7 cuiquam: "to (for) a friend". 8 te: Catullus.
9 quae: haec. ingratae menti: Lesbia's. 10
excrucies: deliberative subjunctive. 11 istinc:
"from that love affair". 12 dis invitis: ablative absolute with concessive force.

qui, qua (quae), quod any
recordor, 1 remember
benefactum, i kindness
prior, prius earlier, former
voluptas, atis, f. pleasure
cogito, 1 think
pius, a, um dutiful
sanctus, a, um holy
violo, 1 violate
foedus, deris, n. compact
divus, i god
fallo, 3, fefelli, falsum deceive
numen, minis, n. majesty,
  divinity
abutor, 3, abusus misuse
5 paro, 1 obtain, earn
longus, a, um long
aetas, atis, f. age, lifetime
ingratus, a, um unrequited,
  thankless
gaudium, ii joy

quicumque, quaecumque,
  quodcumque whoever,
  whatever
quisquam, quidquam anyone,
  anything
pereo, perire, perii, peritum
  perish, be lost
credo, 3, credidi, creditum
  entrust, lend
10 quare wherefore
amplius longer, more
excrucio, 1 torture
quin why not
offirmo, 1 firm up,
  make resolute
istinc thence
reduco, 3, reduxi, reductum
  lead back
dis = deis
invitus, a, um unwilling
desino, 3, desii, desitum cease
miser, a, um wretched

"It was Ben Jonson who was to realize more completely than any other Elizabethan the full value of the pictures drawn by Catullus"—James A. S. McPeek, *Catullus in Strange and Distant Britain* (Cambridge, Mass., 1939), p. 191.

"For a poet who borrowed ideas freely wherever they appealed to him, Shakespeare manifests an astonishing independence of Catullus in his songs and sonnets"— McPeek, *op. cit.*, p. 51.

Difficile est longum subito deponere amorem;
  difficile est, verum hoc qualibet efficias.
15 Una salus haec est, hoc est tibi pervincendum;
  hoc facias, sive id non pote, sive pote.
O di, si vestrum est misereri, aut si quibus umquam
  extrema iam ipsa in morte tulistis opem,
me miserum aspicite et, si vitam puriter egi,
20   eripite hanc pestem perniciemque mihi.
Heu, mihi subrepens imos ut torpor in artus
  expulit ex omni pectore laetitias!
Non iam illud quaero, contra me ut diligat illa,
  aut, quod non potis est, esse pudica velit:
25 ipse valere opto et taetrum hunc deponere morbum.
  O di, reddite mi hoc pro pietate mea.

---

14 efficias: jussive subjunctive; so, too, facias
in line 16. 16 pote (est). 17 si vestrum
est misereri: "if pity is your attribute". 20
pestem perniciemque: "deadly love-sickness".
mihi: dative of separation. ut: "how!" mihi: dative of possession after artus. 22 omni:
logically modifies laetitias. 23 illa: Lesbia.
24 quod: "because". est: subject of est (and
velit) is Lesbia. 26 hoc: the wish expressed
in line 25.

...
...

difficilis, e difficult
subito suddenly
depono, 3, deposui, depositum
   put aside
verum but
qualibet in any way you please
efficio, 3, effeci, effectum
   accomplish
15 salus, utis, f. means of
   deliverance
pervinco, 3, pervici, pervictum
   bring about with difficulty
sive…sive whether…or
potis, e possible, able
di = dei
misereor, 2, misertus pity
quis, quid anyone, anything
umquam ever
extremus, a, um last, final
ops, opis, f. help
aspicio, 3, aspexi, aspectum
   look upon
puriter uprightly
ago, 3, egi, actum spend
20 eripio, 3, eripui, ereptum
   take away

pestis, is, f. disease
pernicies, iei, f. calamity
heu alas!
subrepo, 3, subrepsi,
   subreptum creep
imus, a, um inmost
torpor, oris, m. lethargy
artus, us, m. joint
expello, 3, expuli, expulsum
   drive out
pectus, toris, n. heart
laetitia, ae joy
quaero, 3, quaesivi,
   quaesitum ask
contra in return
diligo, 3, dilexi, dilectum love
pudicus, a, um chaste
volo, velle, volui wish
25 valeo, 2, valui, valitum be well
opto, 1 wish
taeter, tra, trum foul
morbus, i disease
reddo, 3, reddidi,
   redditum grant
pietas, atis, f. piety

"His great virtue is sincerity. Strong and simple
utterance is given to deep feeling, whether love
or hate for Lesbia, sorrow for his brother, or rap-
ture over a friend's home-coming; he ranks with
Sappho and Shelley among the greatest lyric poets
of all time"—A. M. Duff in *Oxford Classical Dic-
tionary* (1950).

70. A Woman's Words

Nulli se dicit mulier mea nubere malle
    quam mihi, non si se Iuppiter ipse petat.
Dicit: sed mulier cupido quod dicit amanti
    in vento et rapida scribere oportet aqua.

75. Quandary

Huc est mens deducta tua, mea Lesbia, culpa,
    atque ita se officio perdidit ipsa suo,
ut iam nec bene velle queat tibi, si optima fias,
    nec desistere amare, omnia si facias.

85. Paradox

Odi et amo.Quare id faciam fortasse requiris.
    Nescio, sed fieri sentio et excrucior.

METER: elegiac couplet (-xx/-xx/-xx/-xx/-xx/--)
                            (-xx/-xx/-/-xx/-xx/-)

INFLUENCE: 70: Richard Brome, "Northern Lass";
John Donne, "The Expostulation."
85: Spenser, "Amoretti," 42,1-4;
Gascoigne, "A Strange Passion of a Lover."

NOTES: 70: 1 nulli: dative after nubere.
mulier: Lesbia. 3 mulier: subject of dicit.
The quod clause is the object of scribere.
75: 1 tua: modifies culpa. 2 ipsa: mens.
3 (mens) queat. **85:** 2 (id) fieri.

70 mulier, eris, f. woman
nubo, 3, nupsi, nuptum marry
malo, malle malui prefer
quam but
Iuppiter, Iovis, m. Jupiter
peto, 3, petii, petitum
seek, woo
cupidus, a, um eager
amans, antis, m. lover
ventus, i wind
rapidus, a, um running
scribo, 3, scripsi, scriptum
write
oportet, 2, oportuit it is fit

75 huc to this pass
deduco, 3, deduxi, deductum
reduce
culpa, ae fault
officium, ii devotion
perdo, 3, perdidi, perditum
ruin

bene volo, velle, volui wish
one well
queo, quire, quii, quitum
be able
optimus, a, um best
fio, fieri, factus become
desisto, 3, destiti,
destitum cease

85 odi, odisse hate
quare why
fortasse perhaps
requiro, 3, requisivi,
requisitum ask
nescio, 4, nescii, nescitum
know not
fio, fieri, factus happen
sentio, 4, sensi, sensum feel
excrucio, 1 torment

SHAKESPEARE

Cymbeline III,v, 70

I love and hate her; for she's fair and royal,
And that she hath all courtly parts, more exquisite
Than lady, ladies, woman; from every one
The best she hath, and she, of all compounded,
Outsells them all. I love her therefore; but
Disdaining me and throwing favours on
The low Posthumus slanders so her judgment
That what's else rare is chok'd; and in that point
I will conclude to hate her, nay, indeed,
To be reveng'd upon her.

86. Fairest of the Fair

Quintia formosa est multis; mihi candida, longa,
    recta est—haec ego sic singula confiteor,
totum illud 'formosa' nego; nam nulla venustas,
    nulla in tam magno est corpore mica salis.
5 Lesbia formosa est, quae cum pulcherrima tota est,
    tum omnibus una omnes surripuit Veneres.

87. No Love Like Mine

Nulla potest mulier tantum se dicere amatam
    vere, quantum a me Lesbia amata mea est.
Nulla fides ullo fuit umquam foedere tanta,
    quanta in amore tuo ex parte reperta mea est.

METER: elegiac couplet (-xx/-xx/-xx/-xx/-xx/--)
                    (-xx/-xx/-/-xx/-xx/-)

INFLUENCE: 86: Shakespeare, "Love's Labour's
Lost", II,i,9; "The Tempest", III,i,39.

NOTES: 86: 1 multis: "In the judgment of many".
candida, longa, recta: characteristics of fem-
inine beauty. 2 haec singula: "these individ-
ual points". 3 totum: functions adverbially:
"wholly". illud 'formosa': "that word 'beautiful" (Ellis). 4 magno: "splendid" rather than
"large". mica salis: "spark of animation" (Ellis). 5 tota: "from head to foot". 6 omnibus
(puellis). **87:** 1 amatam (esse). 4 tuo: "of you".

86 Quintia, ae: Quintia,
       a Roman beauty
    formosus, a, um beautiful
    candidus, a, um fair
    longus, a, um tall
    rectus, a, um straight
    sic thus, so
    singulus, a, um one by one
    confiteor, 2, confessus grant
    totus, a, um whole
    nego, 1 deny
    venustas, atis, f. beauty
    tam so
    corpus, poris, n. body
    mica, ae grain
    sal, salis, m. salt, wit
  5 Lesbia, ae Lesbia (Clodia)
    cum…tum both…and

    pulcher, chra, chrum: beautiful
    unus, a, um alone
    surripio, 3, surripui, surreptum
       steal
    Venus, neris, f. Charm

87 mulier, eris, f. woman
    tantum…quantum so much as
    vere truly
    Lesbia, ae Lesbia (Clodia)
    fides, ei, f. faithfulness
    umquam ever
    foedus, deris, n. pact, bond
    tantus…quantus so great…as
    pars, partis, f. part
    reperio, 4, repperi, repertum
       find

WILLIAM CONGREVE

Epilogue to the Way of the World

For, as when painters form a matchless face,
They from each fair one catch some different grace,
And shining features in one portrait blend,
To which no single beauty must pretend;
So poets oft do in one piece expose
Whole belles assemblees of coquettes and beaux.

101. Ave atque Vale

Multas per gentes et multa per aequora vectus
   advenio has miseras, frater, ad inferias,
ut te postremo donarem munere mortis
   et mutam nequiquam alloquerer cinerem,
5 quandoquidem fortuna mihi tete abstulit ipsum,
   heu miser indigne frater adempte mihi.
Nunc tamen interea haec, prisco quae more parentum
   tradita sunt tristi munere ad inferias,
accipe fraterno multum manantia fletu,
10   atque in perpetuum, frater, ave atque vale.

METER: elegiac couplet (-xx/-xx/-xx/-xx/-xx/--)
                        (-xx/-xx/-/-xx/-xx/-)

INFLUENCE: Herrick, "To the Reverent Shade of His Religious Father"; Swinburne, "Ave atque Vale."

NOTES: 3 te...munere: the verb donare often takes the accusative of the person, the ablative of the thing. donarem: like alloquerer, the secondary tense perhaps to indicate that the intention behind advenio is long conceived. 5 mihi: as in line 6, dative of separation. 7 haec: gifts. 8 tristi munere: "by way of sad service" (a loose ablative). 9 multum: adverb modifying manantia.

gens, gentis, f. nation
aequor, oris, n. sea
veho, 3, vexi, vectum bear,
   convey
advenio, 4, adveni, adventum
   come to
miser, a, um sorrowful,
   wretched
inferiae, arum obsequies,
   funeral sacrifices
postremus, a, um last
dono, 1 present
munus, neris, n. service
mutus, a, um silent
nequiquam in vain
alloquor, 3, allocutus address
cinis, neris, f. ashes
5 quandoquidem since
fortuna, ae fortune
tete = te

aufero, auferre, abstuli,
   ablatum bear off
heu alas!
indigne shamefully
adimo, 3, ademi, ademptum
   take away
interea meanwhile, as things are
priscus, a, um ancient
mos, moris, m. manner
parens, entis, m. father
trado, 3, tradidi, traditum offer
tristis, e sad
accipio, 3, accepi, acceptum
   receive
fraternus, a, um a brother's
mano, 1 flow, drip
fletus, us, m. tears
10 in perpetuum forever
ave hail!
vale farewell!

TENNYSON

Frater Ave atque Vale

Row us out from Desenzano, to your Sirmione row!
So they row'd, and there we landed— 'O venusta Sirmio!'
There to me thro' all the groves of olive in the
summer glow,
There beneath the Roman ruin where the purple
flowers grow,
Came that 'Ave atque Vale' of the Poet's hopeless woe,
Tenderest of Roman poets nineteen hundred years ago....